A Note to Parents

DK READERS is a compelling programme for beginning readers, designed in conjunction with leading literacy experts, including Maureen Fernandes, B.Ed (Hons). Maureen has spent many years teaching literacy, both in the classroom and as a specialist in a school.

Beautiful illustrations and superb full-colour photographs combine with engaging, easy-to-read stories to offer a fresh approach to each subject in the series. Each DK READER is guaranteed to capture a child's interest while developing his or her reading skills, general knowledge and love of reading.

The five levels of DK READERS are aimed at different reading abilities, enabling you to choose the books that are exactly right for your child:

Pre-level 1: Learning to read
Level 1: Beginning to read
Level 2: Beginning to read alone
Level 3: Reading alone
Level 4: Proficient readers

The "normal" age at which a child begins to read can be anywhere from three to eight years old. Adult participation through the lower levels is very helpful for providing encouragement, discussing storylines and sounding out unfamiliar words.

No matter which level you select, you can be sure that you are helping your child learn to read, then read to learn!

For Dorling Kindersley
Senior Slipcase Designer Mark Penfound
Senior DTP Designer Kavita Varma
Producer David Appleyard
Managing Editor Sadie Smith
Managing Art Editor Ron Stobbart
Creative Manager Sarah Harland
Art Director Lisa Lanzarini
Publisher Julie Ferris
Publishing Director Simon Beecroft

Reading Consultant Maureen Fernandes

For Lucasfilm
Executive Editor J. W. Rinzler
Art Director Troy Alders
Keeper of the Holocron Leland Chee
Director of Publishing Carol Roeder

Designed and edited by Tall Tree Ltd
Designers Richard Horsford and
Malcolm Parchment
Editor Catherine Saunders

This edition published in 2015
First published in Great Britain in 2013 by
Dorling Kindersley Limited,
80 Strand, London, WC2R 0RL

This edition produced for The Book People,
Hall Wood Avenue, Haydock, St. Helens WA11 9UL

Slipcase UI: 001–291320–Oct/15

Page design copyright © 2015 Dorling Kindersley Limited.
A Penguin Random House Company

© and TM 2015 LUCASFILM LTD.

A CIP catalogue record for this book
is available from the British Library

ISBN: 978-1-4093-2548-2

Printed in China.

www.starwars.com
www.dk.com

A WORLD OF IDEAS:
SEE ALL THERE IS TO KNOW

Contents

DK READERS

STAR WARS™

BOUNTY HUNTERS FOR HIRE

Written by
Catherine Saunders

What is a bounty hunter?

A bounty hunter is far worse than most other galactic rogues, such as smugglers or pirates. Smugglers transport goods or people around illegally, while pirates steal spaceships.

Smugglers
A crime lord and an evil Sith have hired bounty hunters to find these smugglers, Han Solo and Chewbacca.

Bounty hunters are much more dangerous. A bounty hunter's job is to catch a special kind of prey – people. He or she will capture or even destroy anyone for a special fee, which is called a bounty.

Let's find out about all the most dangerous bounty hunters in the galaxy.

Jetpack

Jango Fett

Meet one of the best bounty hunters in the galaxy. Jango Fett is strong, tough and cunning. First he carefully tracks his prey, then he captures them. He is also a skilled fighter, which is useful if his prey does not want to surrender.

Wrist gauntlet

Knee pad

Every soldier looks, thinks and fights exactly like Jango Fett.

Jango Fett is so tough that he was chosen to be the template for an enormous clone army. Every soldier is a clone, or copy, of the feared bounty hunter.

Jetpack
Jango carries many deadly weapons. His jetpack enables him to fly short distances. It is armed with three missiles.

In action

A bounty hunter must do whatever it takes to complete his or her mission. For Jango Fett that means fighting Jedi Knight Obi-Wan Kenobi.

Jango Fett is a tough fighter, but Obi-Wan is no ordinary opponent. Fett will need all his secret weapons in this battle.

Obi-Wan is skilled
with the Jedi weapon,
known as a lightsaber.

The bounty hunter uses his
blasters, his flame thrower and
his jetpack, but Obi-Wan
will not be beaten. Finally,
Fett distracts the Jedi
Knight just long
enough to escape.

Jetpack

Blaster

Zam Wesell

Blaster

Bounty hunters don't take sides – they'll work for whoever pays them the most money. Clawdite bounty hunter Zam Wesell is sent to destroy a politician called Senator Amidala. If Zam succeeds, it could lead to war.

Zam Wesell looks human, but she isn't.

However, Zam isn't concerned about the fate of the galaxy, or its people. Destroying a galactic senator is simply a job to her. Bounty hunters like Zam don't care who has hired them and they rarely ask why.

Helmet

This is Zam's true appearance. She is a Clawdite shapeshifter.

Code of honour

Bounty hunters have an honour code called the Bounty Hunter's Creed. It states that they should destroy only when necessary and that they should never attack another hunter. However, some bounty hunters follow the creed only when it suits them.

Zam jumps in her airspeeder
to flee from the Jedi, but
they catch her.

Zam fails to eliminate Senator
Amidala. Instead she is pursued
by two Jedi Knights, so Jango
Fett eliminates her.

Airspeeder

Zam Wesell pilots
a Koro-2 exodrive
airspeeder. It is perfect
for making speedy getaways.

Boba Fett

This is the most famous bounty hunter in the galaxy – and also one of the deadliest. His name is Boba Fett and he is a cunning tracker, an expert marksman and a determined fighter. Boba is the son of another bounty hunter, Jango Fett.

Jetpack

Cloak

Boba Fett is actually a clone of Jango
Fett, but Jango raised him as a son.

If Boba sets out to track and
capture someone, he usually
succeeds. He has been on many
dangerous missions and his
armour bears the scars of many
fierce battles.

Slave I
This ship first belonged
to Jango Fett. Boba
added an ion cannon
and a miniature
tractor-beam projector.

Jabba the Hutt

Often evil creatures prefer to do business with bounty hunters. Jabba the Hutt is a huge, slimy gangster who lives on the desert planet Tatooine. He is rich, powerful and very cruel.

Slimy, green skin

Han owes Jabba credits after a smuggling
job went wrong.

Jabba lives in a palace and
runs a vast criminal empire.
He is greedy but very lazy.
Jabba uses bounty hunters to do
the jobs that he would rather
not do himself. He hires
Boba Fett to find the
smuggler Han Solo, who
owes him credits.

Dangerous job

Bounty hunting is a dangerous business. If a bounty hunter is on your trail, he will probably find you. However, sometimes, in a battle to capture his or her prey, a bounty hunter might lose...

Greedo works for
Jabba the Hutt.

Rodian bounty hunter Greedo
wants to claim the bounty for
Han Solo, so he confronts the
smuggler in a busy cantina.
Greedo pulls out his blaster, but
Han Solo reacts quicker. He wins
a deadly shoot-out and escapes.

Darth Vader

Evil Sith Lord Darth Vader rules the galaxy with Emperor Palpatine. Vader wants to find Han Solo's ship, the *Millennium Falcon*, so he gathers together six deadly bounty hunters.

Darth Vader

Dengar

IG–88

Boba Fett

IG–88

This deadly droid is armed and dangerous. He is programmed to search and destroy.

Whoever finds the ship first will receive the bounty. Each bounty hunter is determined to win.

Bossk

4–LOM

Zuckuss

Bossk

This reptile is one of the most vile bounty hunters in the galaxy.

His name is Bossk and he comes from the violent planet of Trandosha. Many Trandoshans choose to become bounty hunters.

Spare blaster bolts

Scaly skin

Bossk and Boba Fett are bitter rivals. Each one believes he is the better bounty hunter.

Bossk's speciality is hunting Wookiees. Only the fiercest bounty hunter can hunt Wookiees as they are over 2 metres (6 feet 6 inches) tall and extremely strong. The vicious Bossk is currently on the trail of the smuggler Han Solo and his Wookiee co-pilot Chewbacca. He is determined to find them before Boba Fett does.

Jango Fett gives Zam Wesell her orders.

Teaming up

Most bounty hunters prefer to work alone. However, for some missions they need to team up. Jango Fett and Zam Wesell joined forces to try and eliminate Senator Amidala, while 4-LOM and Zuckuss often work together.

In fact, 4–LOM and Zuckuss work better as a team. The droid 4-LOM is highly intelligent, while the insectoid Zuckuss is able to use the powerful Force to track prey.

4–LOM

Zuckuss

Aurra Sing

Some people, such as the Jedi, don't like to work with bounty hunters. The Jedi believe in honour and justice, but bounty hunters work for whoever pays them. However, it is rumoured that bounty hunter Aurra Sing used to be a Jedi.

Mentor

After the death of Jango Fett, Aurra Sing guided young Boba Fett. She taught him how to be a successful bounty hunter.

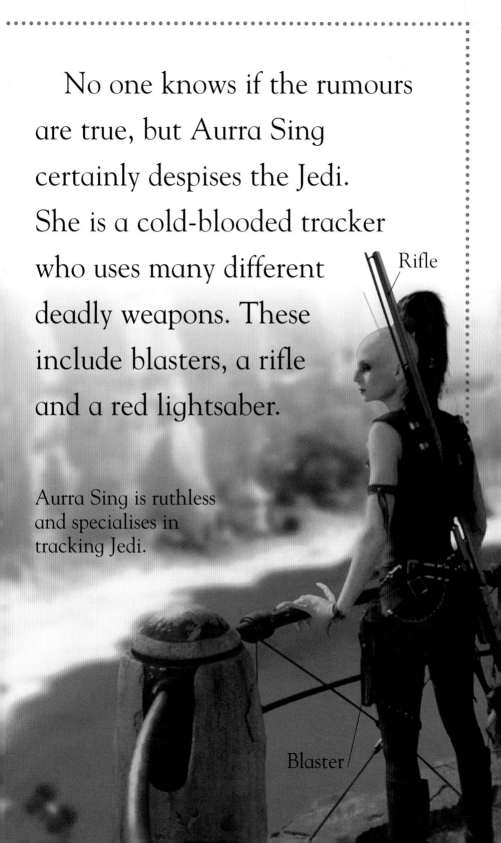

No one knows if the rumours are true, but Aurra Sing certainly despises the Jedi. She is a cold-blooded tracker who uses many different deadly weapons. These include blasters, a rifle and a red lightsaber.

Rifle

Aurra Sing is ruthless and specialises in tracking Jedi.

Blaster

Princess Leia

Not every bounty hunter is exactly what they seem. This bounty hunter is rebel leader Princess Leia, in disguise.

Chewbacca pretends to be Leia's prisoner.

Helmet

Speech scrambler

Rebel princess

Leia is one of the leaders
of the Rebel Alliance.
The rebels want to
restore freedom
to the people
of the galaxy.

Leia is wearing the clothes of
a dead bounty hunter, Boushh,
in order to rescue Han Solo from
Jabba the Hutt. Unlike an
ordinary bounty hunter, Leia is
not being paid. She is risking
her life to save
her friend.

Leia succeeds
in her mission
to rescue Han.

A deadly job

Being a bounty hunter is a very dangerous job. Bounty hunters track, capture and often fight with other people. They usually work alone. Life as a bounty hunter can be hard.

Jango Fett was a great bounty hunter, but his job cost him his life.

Bounty hunters have to be tough and be prepared to risk their lives to complete their missions. They often work for very bad individuals, such as Jabba the Hutt or Darth Vader, and hunt very good individuals, such as Han Solo. Generally things don't end very well for bounty hunters...

Jango Fett was not tough enough to defeat Jedi Master Mace Windu.

Quiz

1. Is Han Solo a pirate?

2. Where is Greedo from?

3. Who lives in a palace on Tatooine?

4. Who likes to hunt Wookiees?

5. Who is disguised as Boushh?

6. Can a droid be a bounty hunter?

Answers: 1. No, he is a smuggler. 2. Rodia 3. Jabba the Hutt 4. Bossk 5. Princess Leia 6. Yes, just ask 4-LOM and IG-88.